# Praise for Carolyn Hobdey's writing

## Redefining SELFISH

*As a busy, working mum of two young daughters, prioritising 'me time' is something of a joke. Carolyn Hobdey guided me through the process of Redefining SELFISH, and it was eye-opening. I admit to the book setting me off down a path I wasn't expecting. The Elimination section was particularly enlightening. I realised that I had got into some bad habits that were damaging to my long-term health (physical and mental). And because Carolyn has been there, done that, got the t-shirt, it never feels patronising or challenging. Her advice is more like sitting with someone kind and wise, straight-talking but with my best interests at heart, written from the heart, to help women like me regain control and balance. Hugely empowering.*
**Amazon reviewer**

*Redefining SELFISH by Carolyn Hobdey is written from the heart.*
**WorkingMums.co.uk**

*This book takes an empathetic approach and gives bitesize approaches, it allows you to have kindness and patience with yourself when dealing with life. This is so necessary for everyone to read in life. Highly recommend. Especially loved the reflection to true life to humanise my feelings and relate.*
**Netgalley reviewer**

*Thought provoking and motivating. Women are traditionally taught (by society) to stay in their boxes, and this book provides motivation to speak up, redefine yourself. SELFISH, in this book, is used to describe various words which helps with redefining yourself.*
**Netgalley reviewer**

*I recommend this book to anyone who is tired of living for others, and not themselves.*
**Netgalley reviewer**

GW00643007

## All The Twats I Met Along The Way

*This is a bold memoir about a woman falling down, getting back up again, and trying time and time again to become a better person. And she's done it.*
**Amazon reviewer**

*The honesty and rawness of Carolyn's words are utterly reassuring. I found myself gripped by her story and better able to assess my own experiences, as I was able to relate to so much of what she had to say.*
**Amazon reviewer**

*Blisteringly, searingly honest. How much crap can one person take in a life? Limitless it seems and yet all of Carolyn's story is told with honesty, anguish, sometimes really funny and sometimes the love shines through. But I did notice there never seemed to be a victim's plea. She literally just got straight back up and moved on. And all the time I wanted to turn the page to find the next Twat. Fabulous stuff.*
**Amazon reviewer**

*An absorbing read. Honest and thoughtful.*
**Amazon reviewer**

*An inspiring, frank and utterly original read that I cannot recommend highly enough.*
**The Book Doctor**

*A word of warning before you start to read this book by Harrogate based Carolyn Hobdey - it is highly addictive. I picked up the book to have a quick look through it at 10pm - by 12.30am I was still engrossed in this true tales of awful boyfriends, manipulating men, love triangles and unsupported medical diagnoses.*
**Lancashire Times**

*Carolyn Hobdey and her books have been featured in i News, Daily Mail, Scottish Daily Mail, Irish Daily Mail, Daily Mirror, The Sun, Woman's Own, Channel 4's Steph's Packed Lunch BBC Radio, WeAreHoi, Lancashire Times, Harrogate Examiner, Yorkshire Times, HR Wire, HR Grapevine, Parenting without Tears, Female First, Working Mums, The Successful Founder, North Manchester FM, Family Friendly Working, The Carer, Netdoctor and more...*

# Redefining

# SELFISH

## CAROLYN HOBDEY

By The Author School

Published by Ink! Publishing 2021

Text @ Carolyn Hobdey 2021
Illustrations @ Helen Braid 2021
Cover Design @ Helen Braid 2021

Typeset in Garamond Classic 11.25/14 by Blaze Typesetting

ISBN number 978-1-7399703-0-7

ink! By The Author School
Kent, England, United Kingdom
Email: inkpublishingservices@gmail.com
Website: www.inkpublishingservices.co.uk
Twitter: @services_ink

*For my niece, Charlotte, and my nephew, George.*
*You inspire me to be a better version of myself every day,*
*so that I might one day inspire you.*

"I can relate to this book in so many ways. Carolyn has written such an empowering book, which not only helps you identify things that we often do to our own detriment to please others but has also given the tools from her own experience to redefine the way we look at ourselves and situations. We must take care of ourselves and wellbeing and Carolyn makes this so easy to understand and re-writing the narrative of selfish being a negative."

**Jess Impiazzi**

*"I worked really hard to find my way back to myself, my **true** self, and I'll never **abandon** her again."*
-@JessNugentı-

# Acknowledgements

It takes more than a writer to create a book. My special thanks goes to:

Helen Lewis for believing in me, cheering me on and keeping me sane throughout the process.

Helen Braid for her beautiful illustrations and Kate Turner's excellent work making it all look lovely.

Clare Clarke for her document designs and to Emma Fletcher, both at Fusion3Media, for getting them on my website.

Gill and George Farr for looking after me whilst I wrote the content (and for challenging me always to ensure I live by my words).

My wonderful early readers who gave me invaluable feedback and encouragement: Rachel Hale and Tina Reid.

To my amazing army of friends who tolerate my endless beating of the drum about being 'S.E.L.F.I.S.H.'

## *Do you recognise yourself here?*

- I feel guilty if I put myself first.

- I juggle numerous demands for my time and attention.

- I consider being selfish to be a bad thing.

- I have an endless 'to do' list and I never reach the bottom of it (where I am).

- I've previously been called 'selfish' for asserting my needs.

- I feel weary, burnt out, resentful and/or undervalued.

- I struggle to prioritise my wellbeing.

- I want practical ways to get started with better looking after my needs.

# CHAPTER 1

## Why did I write this book?

Have you ever been told that you're selfish?

I have.

I grew up with its negative connotations, thinking it was a really bad thing. As I got into adult relationships, the low self-esteem I'd suffered from since childhood meant that my choice of partner was questionable (at best!), so when I failed to please one of those men and he told me I was 'selfish' I took the label on. Somehow, I thought I deserved it; there was a reason why the men in my life treated me as they did and it was—as I thought only natural to assume—my fault.

It was only later (much later) when I realised that all I'd done with that guy (and others) was try to assert my needs. I learnt that difference the hard way. The very hard way. That, however, is a story for a different book. One that I've already written. It was a book about Twats. If you're interested, please look for 'All The Twats I Met Along The Way' online or in your local bookshop.

Before that moment of enlightenment, however, my people-pleasing had gone into overdrive as I did everything possible to not be 'selfish.' As it transpired, being selfless came at huge personal cost. I subjugated my needs for those of others and, increasingly over the decades, saw mine as less important. Don't get me wrong, I wasn't a complete doormat; I had an enviable career and a lifestyle to match. What was going on inside of me wasn't anything to be proud of, however, as I sank further and further into a place of self-loathing with each disastrous relationship encounter.

It was when my home and work lives concurrently imploded in July 2018 that I was forced to take a long, hard look at my life. At me. What was it that had led me to this (dark) place? Who had I been along that road? How had I behaved? What attitudes and mindsets had I cultivated?

The answers were ugly.

In my pursuit of perfection. My desire to care for everyone. To be loved because I believed I was unlovable. To please because I lived out the label of 'selfish'. . . Well, you can probably imagine who I'd become. You may have been that person too. You may be that person right now. If you are, I'm here to tell you it's OK. You're not alone and you don't have to remain this way. I'm here to be the light at the end of the tunnel. We'll walk the rest of the way together. Into the light.

What I'd actually become was faceless. I'd given up so much of my identity to relationship servitude that I'd totally lost sight of who I was. In my snivelling gratitude for anyone who showed me any kind of attention (not to be confused with affection, so I learnt), I'd morphed into whatever they wanted from me to gain their approval in the hope they wouldn't, like everyone who had gone before, leave me. Become another relationship failure.

When I took that deep dive into who I was—the decisions I'd taken, the red flags I'd missed—what I discovered was that a lack of love for myself had allowed me to consistently place myself at the bottom of my priority list. In my work. In my home life. I put everyone else higher up on my list and left no room for me. In particular, there was no place for being kind to me. In fact, the desire to service everyone else's needs meant that I was often quite cruel to me: both in the way I spoke to myself in my head and in how hard I drove myself physically. I was never good enough. I believed I wasn't good enough. Even though the facts of my life told an entirely different story.

I'd had an admirable career working for some of the world's largest employers and some of our most internationally recognised brands. I had a first degree, a Master's degree and various other qualifications under my belt. I'd won prizes for my academic achievements. I'd lived in an impressive Georgian house, owned two cars, had foreign holidays, great friends. . . you get the picture. I don't tell you any of that to sound grand. I tell you because, as I surveyed the ashes of the life I'd lost, I had to ask: what the hell had gone wrong?

It resulted in the stark realisation that there was a need to completely reset my identity. It was time for me to learn to love me. I needed to place myself at the top of my list of problems to solve, matters to attend to and where my time needed to be spent. It was time for me to redefine what I understood 'selfish' to mean.

It was the beginning of a huge transformation. I totally changed my mindset about me and, as a result, my attitude to life.

It was a challenge. I'm not going to sugar-coat it. It would be wrong to mislead you by telling you it was. I was on the self-love wagon. I fell off it. The journey wasn't linear and I went around in a few circles. Old habits crept back in. Sometimes they still do.

Yet, it was the most rewarding thing I've done in my life to date. Some days I cry with the sheer joy, pride and relief at how far I have come. I look different. I sound different. I feel different.

What was the biggest transformational impact? The change in my relationships with those around me. Not least because I got rid of the toxic ones and put my energy into the positive ones. Suddenly, I was better able to be what others needed from me, because I was now a much better version of myself.

So, if you've ever been told you are (or thought yourself to be) selfish or if you're simply someone who struggles to know it's OK to put yourself first. . . then this book is for you. It's high time for some much-needed Tender Loving (self) Care.

# CHAPTER 2

## Why do we see 'selfish' as a bad thing?

Before we set about redefining what we consider to be selfish, let's begin with what it means. Its definition is, inherently, negative:

> *'Concerned excessively or exclusively with oneself: seeking or concentrating on one's own advantage, pleasure, or wellbeing without regard for others.'*
> -merriam-webster.com-

Basically, it's putting yourself first.

So, this is a bad thing? Is making yourself a priority a behaviour for which we should be criticised?

At a foundational level the societal answer is: yes.

There are examples all around us of how we celebrate those who 'selflessly' put everyone else above themselves. The mums who, as Teri Hatcher once wrote, insist that they will eat the burnt toast rather than anyone else having to endure it. The woman who breathlessly arrives at every meeting having allowed herself no time between appointments or gives time to anyone who stops her en route regardless of how that distracts or delays her. The one who permits every interruption, puts whatever she was doing aside and places anything she needs at the bottom of her 'to-do' list; a perpetual list that she never gets to the end of.

Somehow, we praise instead the dicing-with-burnout, trying-to-have-it-all jugglers and hold them up as examples to which us mere mortals should aspire. Then there's the worst of their kind. We've all met them. The gluten-free pillars of virtue. They hold down a brutal job to which they commute whilst listening to the latest self-improvement podcast so that they can tell us about it when they glide gracefully through the office with never a hair out of place or food spilt down their perfectly-pressed blouse. Those that appear to have the ideal home life with beautifully behaved children, who tell you that in their 'spare time' they love to do baking for their neighbours and not only do they do some yoga, they're actually a Certified Practitioner.

Their selflessness is a yardstick with which we beat ourselves for our own ineptitude.

No wonder that the idea of being selfish is seen as abhorrent. Why wouldn't we want to spend our lives at the end of our tethers aspiring to the impossible, huh?

Instead we all silently berate ourselves for thinking, 'bitch' about *that* woman. Come on, admit it.

Yet, I have to wonder whether at times I did appear to be that woman. Ok, so I'm not a yoga practitioner, I've definitely not baked since leaving school and people that bang on about listening to podcasts make me want to scream. But have I been guilty of portraying that air of perfection? Oh yes. Certainly not because I felt perfect. Nor because I was trying to pretend I was. Absolutely not because I wanted to piss anyone off. I just don't think I knew anything other than putting on a brave face, hiding my pain and doing everything possible to be perfect. Back then, that's what I thought being a fully functioning adult entailed.

I'd like to issue a public apology: I'm really sorry if you met me during that time and I was an annoying cow.

I hated me then too. Know that the world of pain you possibly wished upon me was most definitely raining down on my head in private. Please don't feel guilty about that either.

So, we all agree that being constantly self-centred isn't good. Yet, all that avoidance of selfishness that we so diligently apply ourselves to isn't doing us any good either, is it? It's stressing us out, making us tired and layering a whole load of pressure upon us when the world is already a pretty intense place. Oh, and then these days we all feel the need to take photos of our selflessness just to doubly prove to the world how good we are.

Sod that!

Maybe it's time we had a collective rethink about selfish. What do you reckon? Is it time we took back control and redefined it perhaps?

I think so. It's finally time to stop self-loathing and start self-loving.

# CHAPTER 3

*What if we changed our mindset about 'selfish'?*

Back when I was a Human Resources Director in the corporate world, I was given some feedback by one of my team in a 360-degree appraisal process: "Sometimes working for Superwoman can be quite hard".

Wow. That feedback cut deep. I knew exactly what they were getting at.

It took over a decade and a major meltdown before I understood the power of its insight and heeded its warning. I'd thought that the more I did, the better things would get. That somehow, someday I'd reach the bastion of 'togetherness' where the perfection I drove myself towards would be matched by how I felt. That looking and feeling like I had life sussed would co-exist. I thought that this moment would be called 'maturity', 'wisdom' or 'success'. It turned out that my efforts meant I just got progressively more childlike, unwise and internally unsuccessful.

It was my own experience of being a constant 'human doing' (as my best friend puts it) rather than a human being that I had sit up and take notice of when my world caved in. Something drastic needed to change. I was exhausted: physically and emotionally. I was burnt out from the persistent need to satisfy the innumerable demands that were laid upon me by others, for sure, but most especially by me.

That's when I began to change my relationship with selfish.

When everything on which I'd relied in my life was ripped out from beneath me very suddenly, I was forced to pay huge attention to myself. My heart was broken and the pain that came from the emotional trauma was physical in its manifestation. I stopped eating. I stopped sleeping. I had to concentrate on breathing in and out, which felt like it took every last bit of strength I had. I was being tumbled in a downward spiral that seemed as though it would never end and even if it did, I had an awful feeling it would be to land with a body-wrenching thud that might just possibly finish me off. Either discombobulating constant whirling or smashing into the ground: those felt like my only two choices.

Life was making me think only of me. It was without doubt the best and most-needed lesson.

What changed?

It actually started with learning that I mattered.

The number of people who stepped forward when I was at my lowest ebb astounded me. The things they did, the time they spent and the care they showed for me meant I saw for the first time in a long while that I was valued.

That was the first sign: others thought I was important enough to be taken care of. These amazing, smart, kind people believed I was worthy of their efforts. I needed to reciprocate their energy. Show them that they weren't foolish in their endeavours or misplaced with their values; that I valued them as much as they valued me.

What ensued was a gradual discovery that behaving like I had value actually increased my value to others. Rather than taking on more responsibility (my default setting!) and, instead, taking responsibility for taking care of myself, both mentally and physically, I began to find that those who cared for me and who I cared about, became happier. I switched from thinking they were trying to limit me by getting me to stop and pay attention to myself, to understanding that they were looking out for me. Then, when I acted accordingly, it became obvious that those people worried less about me. I had more energy. I laughed more. I was better company. I looked good.

If we show our loved ones that we set (and stick to) our own boundaries, they will accept them too. When we fail to set them, they feel the need to intervene.

None of my change was happening by accident. It was happening by design; albeit that design was more than a bit haphazard to begin with!

The more time I spent with me and on me, the better I became. I made putting myself right the number one thing I had to do; it paid dividends.

I learnt that's what happens when we're 'selfish'. We become 'better'. Better versions of ourselves. Those around us benefit. There isn't any downside. The only losers are the people who don't like this change; our increased standards for ourselves mean they can no longer benefit from our boundaries being blurred, non-existent or easily breached. They tend to slip away from our lives. Sometimes noisily, but they eventually leave. As the saying goes: "Losing toxic people is a win."

There are enormous benefits of a healthy dose of selfish thinking. So much of what 2020/21 has taught us personally and societally through the impacts of the coronavirus pandemic and successive lockdowns, is how important it is to look after ourselves. To be mindful of the signs when we're not feeling right. The importance of taking action to address our needs, because when our lives are stripped bare, we cannot ignore those needs in the same way as we can in the busy-ness of normal life.

Of the many statistics and studies that are starting to emerge as a result of the pandemic, some are truly concerning for women; they highlight the need for us to be prioritising our emotional and physical wellbeing now more than ever:

- Mental health has 'worsened substantially' as a result of the pandemic (by 8.1% on average) with women and young adults hit the hardest (The Health Foundation-June 2020).
- 63% of women reported feeling more anxious (mentalhealth.org.uk).
- A leading UK law firm reported a 122% increase in divorce enquiries from July to October 2020 with an increase in women initiating divorces to 76% from 60% the previous year (BBC.com - December 2020).
- Calls to the Refuge (domestic abuse) helpline were 49% higher than usual (The Health Foundation - June 2020).
- Adults are 55% more likely to develop obesity if they have short sleep duration due to links with motivation and impacts on their hormones (healthline.com).

- Women over the age of 30 have been hit the hardest by the hiring slowdown during the pandemic (GatenbySanderson).
- The decline in mental health is twice as large in women as for men during the pandemic (The Health Foundation - June 2020).
- Women across the UK and Europe currently spend 15 hours per week more than men on unpaid domestic labour (Boston Consulting Group).
- Studies suggest there were fewer women applying for Executive positions during the pandemic (GatenbySanderson).
- A study of women found that poor sleep was linked to 'slower walking, lower grip strength and greater difficulty performing independent activities' (healthline.com).

And most of that has worsened just in the last year.

If I told you that statistically you could lose weight, have a better immune system, improve your sleep quality, look and feel healthier (and probably younger) as a result of being a bit more selfish. . . would you take me up on it?

Of course you would! It's a no-brainer, right?

So, it makes it even more bizarre that we resist being selfish when the evidence to the contrary is so overwhelming.

OK, so let's agree to give up feeling guilty about taking a bit of time out for ourselves, putting ourselves at the top of our list and acknowledging the benefits of making ourselves better. After all, a better us makes those we love happier. Now, that's not selfish, is it?

Right, that's settled. Let's look at how we do it.

# Chapter 4

## S.E.L.F.I.S.H

When I devised the S.E.L.F.I.S.H. model, it was all about having a comprehensive yet straightforward way for women to learn and keep front-of-mind the things they need to attend to. Its purpose is to encourage self-kindness, develop confidence and shift mindsets from harmful to helpful; all whilst seeing these changes as self-improvement rather than reasons for self-flagellation!

My aim is to provide thought-provoking content that will alter your feelings about doing things that are selfish as well as practical steps you can take. With this in mind, there are easy exercises for you to do at the end of each element of the model to get you started, each of which is supported by a downloadable work-sheet, available from my website.

So, for additional inspiration and support with Redefining SELFISH, visit www.carolynhobdey.com.

I hope you enjoy a bit of S.E.L.F.I.S.H. time!

# The S.E.L.F.I.S.H. Model

**S is for Self-worth**

**E is for Elimination**

**L is for Loving life**

**F is for Failure**

**I is for Identity**

**S is for Sexiness**

**H is for Help**

# S.E.L.F.I.S.H

## S is for Self-Worth

As women, we are typically haunted by memories of our school days (teenage girls can be cruel!) and that derisory phrase: "She so loves herself".

When we're trying to find our way through some of the most significant change we ever go through in our lives (puberty is an even bigger bitch than some teenage girls!), lacking confidence in ourselves as a result and jostling to find our place in the hormonal hierarchy of high school, some of the comments we receive really leave their mark.

The thought of being accused of 'loving ourselves' at that stage is abhorrent. We don't want to be accused of self-love, do we? Heavens above, no!

All of those slights and put-downs are designed to make us feel worse about ourselves. However, we know, thanks to the maturity we now have, that in fact it was all about the lack of self-worth and confidence on the part of the perpetrator. At least, we logically know that; it's not always how we emotionally feel about it even decades later though.

We're conditioned early on that self-love is something to be avoided and certainly not something we should let others see that we have.

Well, I say bollocks to that!

As a complete alternative, I love the saying by Mel Robbins that goes: "When you don't put yourself first, you're teaching everyone that you come second."

If you want a constant reminder of that amazing mantra, download it from my website (www.carolynhobdey.com) and put it somewhere you'll see it daily so it will jolt your thoughts: on your fridge, next to your desk, as your phone screensaver. Put this fabulous quote in a prominent place and start living your life in line with it.

What can we do to improve our sense of self-worth?

I asked that question when I realised my sense of my own value was what had been influencing my life for decades. I thought that my low self-esteem was just part of 'who I am' and was even apologetic for the fact that this was the way I was. I mean, really?! I got a big wake-up call when I was able to look back across the story of my life and see that operating from a place of limited self-worth meant that I had allowed many of the toxic people (and poor situations I had found myself in) to both be allowed into and remain in my life. That's not to say that I was responsible for those people's behaviour—far from it—that was 'their bad', as the saying goes, but I had to examine what it was about my own mindset that attracted and then tolerated those people.

The truth is, I was grateful that they were choosing to be

with me. I felt like they deserved better than me and that them being there was doing me a favour, extending a kindness to me, something for which they should be thanked. Even when I knew that their behaviour was unacceptable, I didn't have it in me to remove them from my life because I believed that no-one else would want me. Having them in my life, despite all the negativity that brought, was preferable to what I thought would surely be a lifetime of loneliness.

That story started in my childhood and it's the stories we tell ourselves that I want to begin with here. With your stories.

The stories that we tell ourselves have a huge impact on our thoughts, our behaviours and our decisions, as well as the relationships we have with others. Yet, when was the last time you examined those stories, where they originate from and the effects they have on your life? Probably a long time ago, if ever. Even if you have looked at it, it's difficult to do and often we don't take the process all the way to its conclusion. It can feel overwhelming trying to find an answer. I know that all too well.

That's where we're going to begin with improving your self-worth, by looking at the stories that you tell yourself. This is because, in my experience, we carry those stories with us; they inform our view of ourselves as well as influencing what we do and the decisions we make. Often more than we realise. Usually, our stories sit in our subconscious, which means that we're unaware of the implications of their work in the background of our minds. What they are busy doing, however, is creating those voices that tell us when they perceive 'danger' from which we should flee (emotionally and physically); this may have been an effective self-protection mechanism in our primal brains but can be a bit less reliable in the more evolved world that those brains are now coping with.

Similarly, those stories help us to look for evidence that reinforces them. This is done at the exclusion of contrary evidence. It turns out that we prefer to be right about our beliefs, so we are happy to discount anything that may prove us wrong, even when that evidence may be compelling and repeated. Therefore, we need to be aware that it may take quite a shake for us to sit up and consciously argue with our subconscious in order to set its record straight.

Finally, our stories have frequently been around for a long time. Our beliefs are typically set in place by the time we are seven years old, so we have to expect that we'll cling to them like a favourite toy and see them as a source of comfort; something on which we rely and return to, especially when times are tough. For this reason we have to expect that changing our stories won't be easy; it's going to take effort, coaxing and repetition, a bit like weening a child off their comfort blanket! Be kind to yourself whilst you're making this change. Hell, be kind to yourself when you're making ANY change!

We'll be looking at how we address our stories in the activity at the end of this section.

In improving our self-worth I want to also examine our self-talk. That is, the words and phrases we use to speak about ourselves in our own head. Another saying I love:

*You will never speak to anyone*
*more than you speak to yourself*
*in your head.*
*Be kind to yourself.*

However, in my experience, both personally and when I talk to friends and colleagues, I discover that we are often very hard on ourselves with what we say in our heads; to the extent of being quite cruel. It's so important that we catch ourselves when we're having these conversations because we become what we think, so when what we think about ourselves is negative. . . well, you can work out the rest for sure.

Examining our self-talk is crucial for improving our self-worth. Whilst it can be cringe-worthy in British culture to stand in front of a mirror and say positive affirmations out loud, I am a firm believer that when we shift the words we say to ourselves in our heads from negative to positive, it can have a massive impact on how we feel. Even if we merely repeat some positive words silently and whether or not that is while looking ourselves straight in the eye in a mirror, as long as we do so consistently then the repetition of those words can be a game-changer. I don't say that lightly. An uplifting statement about ourselves that we go to regularly, but particularly on a bad day or after a difficult meeting or before a conversation that might be tricky, can really change our relationship with ourselves.

If you find it hard to find those words for yourself at this stage, then a good place to start is to ask some people whose opinion you value (and only those types of people) what they would say about you. Take what's useful—rather than just using their words—ingest what resonates with you and then form that into a memorable, short statement. Save it into your phone or somewhere else that you can easily look at it when it's needed. THEN USE IT!

Before we move on from your self-worth, I want to take

some time to look at gaining some perspective. What I mean by that is to create some balance in your thinking about yourself. If you were making a judgement about anything else in your life, or about anyone else, you'd probably weigh that up by looking at the pros and cons. Sometimes, you might make a list of those, but even if you didn't, you'd conduct a bit of a 'checks and balances' exercise in your mind. Yet we rarely afford ourselves that deliberation. I want to encourage you to do that. We'll look more at failures when we get to the 'F' word later on, but right now it is just about knowing that there *should* be balance in how you think about yourself.

Time to make a list (I do love a list, I must confess). On one half of a piece of paper write down everything negative that you think about yourself as you are today. Every last thing. Get it all down. Wring out every last drop of it. Now on the other half of the page, for every negative thought or feeling write a positive one about you. Don't stop until your lists are equal. I'm trusting you here to be honest about that.

Done?

Good. That's what I mean by balance. If your positive list became longer than your negative one then you get a gold star; that's the only kind of imbalance I'm prepared to accept and so should you.

When we don't feel like we're worthy, we tend to think we don't deserve to care for ourselves. That's when your 'to do' list takes over and contains everyone else except you, or you're something that you'll 'get around to eventually'.

What does self-care even mean? Self-care is the practice of consciously doing things that preserve or improve your mental or physical health (source: BMI Healthcare).

Self-care trends have been slowly growing in popularity over recent years, but the successive lockdowns of the coronavirus pandemic have accelerated interest in strategies to care for ourselves when times are tough. If you're reading this book, I'm guessing you may have dipped your toe in the water, but probably not embraced any of the opportunities with gusto or consistently. Perhaps you don't have time for that nonsense. . .

OK, let's change that.

The great thing about self-care is that there are no rules. No-one can tell you what it means to you because it's a very individual thing, so you get to choose what you do and how you do it. The point is that I'm here to encourage you—make that TELL you—to do something. Let's not add to the overwhelm in your busy life (after all, this is meant to be pleasurable!) so don't make the activity onerous, but it does need to be time out that you take for yourself on a regular basis to recharge your battery. And no, that doesn't mean just going to bed at night.

If you struggle to think about what a self-care practice might mean for you, here are some suggestions:

- **Go for a walk**: if you're able to, walk briskly to get your heart rate up and improve your circulation. Do this with a friend for some company and added feel-good that you're replacing time texting with talking face to-face
- **Have a bath**: no, not the type designed to just get you clean. A relaxing one with bubble bath, candles or a book. Schedule this in both with yourself and people in your household, so that they know this is protected

time for you. If you think you can't find time, monitor how much time you spend on social media each day and steal some of those 'wasted' minutes.

- **Prioritise sleep**: this might seem obvious or like the kind of advice your mum would give you, but even just an extra hour of quality sleep can significantly improve our mental and physical health; it's scientific fact. Improve the quality of your sleep by avoiding 'screen time' an hour before bed.

- **Listen to music you love**: even better, dance around to it. If there are others in your home, get them involved. Everyone gets to pick a favourite track that you all dance to. Do this during a break from work or the housework or to mark the start of the weekend. Find an excuse. Exercise and endorphins combined; what's not to love?

- **Cook together**: whether you live by yourself and invite friends over (perhaps via video technology) or you do it with those you live with, making some food together takes the pressure off whoever is usually responsible for cooking. It can be fun and you might all learn a new recipe you love. Making something healthy is even better. Getting others involved also makes the clearing up more bearable!

- **Meditation**: now scientifically proven to have health benefits, meditation has grown in popularity over recent years and is advocated for its success in managing stress and anxiety. In just 10 minutes a day (yes, I think you might struggle to say you can't find time for that) you can become more centred, calm and feel like you've done something just for you. There are lots of free or low-cost Apps you can download with guided meditations for all sorts of situations. Just give it a go.

Of course, self-care is deeper than just doing something nice for yourself. It's about the way you think and it's about doing good things consistently. Yet, what these starter ideas show is that self-care doesn't have to be complicated, costly or consume much of your time. My best advice is to integrate them into your pre-existing routine so that you are reminded to do them regularly and it doesn't feel like another 'thing' to do.

The benefits of self-care are now being widely recognised. Amongst these are the impacts on the quality of our relationships (self-care isn't selfish), the reduction in anxiety (essential given the pandemic experience) and demonstrable improvements in mental and physical health. Why wouldn't we want that for ourselves? Why wouldn't the people who love us want that for us too? If anyone around you makes you feel bad for taking time out for yourself, I suggest you change the people around you, but that's me getting ahead of myself and into the second part of the S.E.L.F.I.S.H. model! Right, before we reach the end of this section by you completing the activity I've prepared for you, I want to finish with some questions for you to reflect on. Ask yourself:

- What is the yardstick against which I'm measuring my self-worth?
- Is there a standard I'm aspiring to? What is that standard and why does it exist?
- Who set that standard? Is it an expectation I have or as

it put there by someone else? Did they have the right to put it there?

Just a few things for you to consider in the pursuit of being kinder to yourself.

## S is for Self-worth
## Activity

*How to speak kindly to yourself*

Make a note of how often in a week you engage in negative self-talk.

Record each day when it happens as well as the content. Understanding what triggers this negativity will enable you to address it.

For a document to complete this activity as well as further **self-worth** resources, find them at: www.carolynhobdey.com/RedefiningSELFISH/Resources

# S.E.L.F.I.S.H

## E is for Elimination

In the last section, I gave you a bit of a hint about what 'Elimination' entails; it's about removing from your life those things that bring you down. Anything or anyone that detracts from you, your happiness, your wellbeing, and from living your life in the way and as the person you want to be. In particular, it is about eliminating those people that are toxic.

OK, so I accept that elimination sounds a bit 'assassin'. For legal reasons I want to state that I'm not recommending that anyone has anyone murdered, or even harmed for that matter. I am talking about removing them from your life or reducing their influence on you.

Why is this important?

The people we surround ourselves with say a lot about who we are and what we think about ourselves. They are a reflection of us in some way, shape or form. Think about that for a moment. What would the people around you communicate to others about who you are? Particularly, what would they demonstrate about the value you place on yourself?

When we place low value on ourselves, we are often prepared to tolerate people who are negative: about the world, about their life and about us. It may not always be that obvious. Yet, we hear ourselves say things like, 'Oh, that's just how they are'. We make excuses for their poor behaviour because we think we either deserve it or we're afraid to address it with them.

Why do we have that fear?

Often, we don't face into other's unacceptable treatment of us because we're afraid of the consequences. We're scared that those consequences will be that they'll leave us. We're fearful of being left because our brains are, as I mentioned previously, still existing in quite a primeval state despite how much we've evolved. We have to remember that back when our ancestors roamed the Savannah, that only those that belonged to the group survived. Being outcast from that group was literally the difference between life and death. Hence why our need to 'belong' can be so compelling. It helps to understand why the need to not be cast out is so strong in so many of us and why getting us to face into that fear can be such a challenge.

Yet, valuing ourselves, doing what is right for us, requires us to examine the people in our life and to take steps to remove those who don't meet the standard we have for the way in which we should be treated. Which starts with us setting that standard. Now, I accept that it might not always be possible to remove these detractors completely from our life. If that person is a close family member, for example, or part of one of our key friendship groups, then just stepping away from them might not be an action we can reasonably take. There are, however, things that you can do, so we're going to take a look at those in this section.

First, let's start by looking at the areas of your life. I like to place our lives into compartments to help to make sense of it and who might be where. I get that life isn't as simple as sitting in neat boxes, but we all categorise our world in order to make sense of it (otherwise our brains would explode with all the disorderly information they would be taking in) so I'm not going to make any apology for trying to make things easier to understand. After all, we're aiming to be kind to ourselves here, aren't we?

I use eight Key Life Areas to help me and my clients to think systematically about the different parts of their world. These areas are:

 **Finance**: steps you take to ensure your financial security.

 **Health & Fitness**: activities you do to attend to your physical health.

 **Spiritual/Emotional Wellbeing**: things you do to look after your mental health.

 **Personal Relationships**: basically, a euphemism for sex and love - your most intimate relationship (or relationships, we're not judging here).

 **Career/Business**: any 'work' activity whether or not it is for financial profit.

**Family & Home life**: immediate and extended home environments.

 **Education/Personal Development**: how you grow your knowledge or learn new skills.

 **Social & Recreation**: friends, hobbies and non-work activities or interests.

The action I want you to take is to look at each of these eight areas and write down the key people you interact with in each one of them. Make those lists first.

For the framework to do this exercise use the document 'Eight Key Life Areas Assessment: How to review the people in your life' at www.carolynhobdey.com to record your answers. Here you will also find a 10-point scale from 'joyful' to 'toxic'.

You've no doubt guessed that I want you to plot all of the people from your lists onto this scale. Now, if this is going to work, you're going to have to be really honest with yourself about where everyone falls. Think about your interactions with each person. Consider those interactions as both actual (you meet them, talk on the phone or video call) or virtual (you think about them or text them); both those forms of communication will influence how each person makes you feel. In placing each key person on the scale, I need you to connect emotionally with how they leave you feeling most often after your contact with them. As you do this, I want you to know that there is no need for you to share any of this with anyone else. You don't need to store your results and you can burn (safely) the piece of paper afterwards. So, this is just between you and you, so be totally honest with yourself. After all, we're practising being selfish, aren't we?

Once you have that picture of where each key person in your life falls along that scale you can start to make some decisions about what to do next. Remember: doing nothing is still a decision, so even if right now isn't the time to tackle a particular person or situation, that is still within your gift to choose. The purpose here is to gain clarity about who and where the issues are, so that you can understand how toxicity in one part of your life might be leaking into others, rather than just living with a feeling of general malaise.

What can you do about those in the toxic half of the scale?

When it comes to elimination, there are levels of the process of removal. These levels will also help you to implement what I was encouraging you to do earlier with regards to setting boundaries. Let's start with something straightforward and work our way towards the more challenging options.

- **Mute notifications**: a really simple one to deploy on social media platforms for individuals or groups. You can do this without them knowing, usually with the option of doing so permanently or just for a fixed period, if you merely want some 'time out' from the negative chatter. We usually know who these people are, the ones who fill our thread with moaning and attention-seeking 'sadfishing'. Quieten them down!
- **Unfollow**: potentially more obvious than muting, but if they are constantly being negative in your feed, why not cut it out altogether by unfollowing or blocking them. Especially as they may be a 'pseudo-friend': someone

who you are connected with on social media, but never actually meet. If they are someone you see and they raise your unfollow with you, just let them know you were doing a bit of social media 'housekeeping' and that you have other ways of staying in touch with them.

- **Minimise them**: this can be done physically or mentally. Spend less time with toxic people either in person or in your mind. Catch yourself if you're ruminating about them. Consciously fill your mind with something else such as thinking something positive about you rather than their negativity. When it comes to 'in person' contact then find ways to see less of them or if they cannot be avoided (family or close friendship group) make sure you don't get stuck with them in social settings. This is about being kind to you, so don't feel bad if you position yourself elsewhere at a dinner table or spend less time talking to them.

- **Tell them**: I understand this is more challenging. However, it's important that you know there is an option to speak to them about their behaviour and the impact it's having on you. Some people might not know the effect they have (on you or others) and might actually appreciate your honesty and the chance to change. Obviously, it's important that you're constructive in your comments: focus on talking about examples of their behaviour and its results rather than getting personal about them. Make sure they are aware that if there isn't a change then you will have to reduce your time in their company (and stick to this!).

- **Create boundaries**: this relates to the points above,

but it's worth calling out in its own right. This is about setting out your standards for how you expect to be treated and living up to them; both privately with yourself and also in any of the actions or conversations you more publicly take. Don't let 'being nice' or guilt make you drop those standards for the sake of others. If others are not prepared to accept your boundary, then see it as confirmation that the boundary needs to be in place. Be aware that they are likely to make it hard for you to maintain the boundary, so anticipate this; think about what you'll do or say so that you have your response pre-determined. This will help to maintain your resolve. Ask yourself: who is benefiting from my current lack of boundaries with them? Who is taking advantage of me? What is the standard that is being breached? Why might that be the case? What can I do about it? There is always something you can do, trust me. Tough questions, but necessary and the answers might be very revealing (and might just strengthen your resolve).

- **Remove them**: walking away from people in your life is hard. I've done it and know it can be heart-breaking at the time, so I'm not being flippant when I suggest this option, I promise you. Sometimes it is undoubtedly the right thing to do. For you, for those around you who feel the effects upon you of that toxic person, and sometimes even for that person themselves. If you're each not making each other happy then removing yourself from their life might also be the best thing for them. One of you has to have the strength to do it, so why not let that be you? This toxic person might be a partner, a boss, a long-standing friend. . . all of these and others are equally as difficult to remove. In these instances there are two things you need:

1. Clear resolve that the end result is the right one for you, which comes from you visualising what it will look and feel like to not have this person's negative influence in your life.
2. A plan for how you're going to make this happen. Break it down into the small steps you need to take to make it happen, then take one step at a time.

You need to know that the difficulty you're feeling whilst going through this change won't last. As the saying goes, 'This too will pass'.

Having completed the above exercise with the people in your life, it's worth going through a similar thought process in two other related areas:

- What are the negative *situations* that you need to change? In which of the eight Key Life Areas do they occur? What actions can you take to change them?
- What are the negative *emotions* that you experience that you need to shift? How often do they occur? What triggers them? What can you do to transform that emotion from negative to positive?

The honesty and self-reflection needed for this section of the model is hard, but I promise you it will be worthwhile; it is a key part of defining who you want to be and how you want to live your life in a more positive way going forwards. I have a final question about elimination for you to reflect upon before you move forward to the next stage of the S.E.L.F.I.S.H. model (although before you do, I'd like you to do something from your self-care list please).

If you're feeling guilty about being 'selfish', especially if this relates to the actions you've identified above about the people in your life, I'd like you to ask yourself: whose guilt is this? It's worth considering whether that guilt is placed upon you by you, or has it been cultivated by someone else. If it's the latter look at why and what that person gains from your guilt.

Right, time for that self-care. . .

## E is for Elimination
## Activity

*How to increase your positivity*

Write a list every day for a week of the emotions you feel that day.

Separate them into columns of positive and negative feelings and state what percentage of your time you spent in each emotion type.

For a document to complete this activity as well as further **elimination** resources, find them at: www.carolynhobdey. com/ RedefiningSELFISH/Resources

S.E.L.F.I.S.H

*L is for Loving life*

In this third section, I want to talk about your life. More accurately, I want to get you to think about the life you'd love.

Most of us drift through life because we have an illusion of time. We have this warped perception that its infinite; that we've got loads of it. Even though we know at the same time that none of us lives forever. That's weird when you think about it. The reality is that none of us knows how much time we actually have. How much life will we truly get to live?

Sadly, it's only when something catastrophic happens in our lives that we absolutely understand that our time is not decided by us and will indeed come to an end, and then we wake up from this illusory stupor. Maybe someone close to us dies—often unexpectedly, without a chance to say our 'goodbyes'—or we ourselves get a brush with death through an accident or a serious medical scare. Only when we're faced with this, even though our logical brains know that any of these could be a possibility at any moment in our immediate future, do we appreciate the limits of our time.

So, why do we take our lives so for granted? It was when I stared square on at own mortality that I started to see that I'd been wasting so much precious time. Worse still, it happened to me because I'd been prepared to bring that mortality abruptly forward; that's how much I'd valued MY life!

It was a huge turning point and one for which I will always so grateful that I got the chance to change. Don't get me wrong, I don't now fill every possible minute of every day with something meaningful and valuable—that just wouldn't be realistic (and just how annoying would that make me?!)— yet my attitude to life has altered dramatically as a result. It changed in the following ways:

- **I assessed what I wanted to achieve in my life.** What I wanted to be able to say about my life: how I lived it, who I was, what I achieved by being here. I wanted to leave a legacy in my tiny patch of the world and I wanted it to be a positive imprint, mostly on the people who came into contact with me, from that moment onwards.
- **I decided that there were still a lot of miles I wanted to get out of my tank.** That meant I had to start treating my body with greater respect if I wanted it to carry me for those miles. This respect meant that a shift was needed physically and mentally in my attitude to my wellbeing. I had to prioritise those things. So, rather than doing even more, sometimes it would involve me doing less to be able to show myself the kindness I spoke of earlier.

I emphasise that I don't get this right all the time, but I have started living my life with a greater sense of clarity and purpose. Taking less for granted. Most of all, I learnt the huge benefits of selfishness in helping me to enact that change in attitude.

Let's talk about your life.

Do you love it? Do you even *like* it?

My experience is that we get so worn down with everyone else's lives and the priority they take—their needs, wants and demands—that we don't allow conscious consideration of how we feel about those questions. Often, it's because their contemplation might be a bit depressing. Worse still, we might actually have to hold ourselves to account for making changes if we didn't like what we saw. After all, what kind of person would we be if we thought our lives were a bit crap and then we didn't do anything about it? See, more pressure. More self-flagellation. See how easy it is to inflict self-harm? If your life isn't what you want and you've not done anything about it, you're in good company:

> *'More than 50% of people don't*
> *have a clear picture of their future and*
> *how they're going to get there.'*
> -Jim Bright, LinkedIn-

This means we can stop being so hard on ourselves, but it doesn't mean I'm going to let you off the hook. I'm going to hold your feet to the flames (don't worry, I'm not going to let it get too hot) whilst we take a look at what you want out of your life and how you might want to start claiming that.

One of my passions is that we all have the right to live the life that's right for us. So often we do what we think we *should* rather than what we *desire* because we fear other's judgement. The reality is, that's just us thinking we're more important to them then we actually are. We're all the centre of our own universe and whilst we're busy occupying ourselves with worries about what other people think of us, the truth is they're not giving us a second thought. We take up none of their mental capacity. Sorry if that burst your bubble. It doesn't mean you don't matter. You do. Enormously. You're important, but my point is that you need to be important to you first and foremost.

In which case, let's put on our big girl pants and ask ourselves some questions about our lives.

The exercise that I'm going to ask you to do at the end of this section is about making a comparison between the life you have and the life you want. I've said this before, but I'm going to repeat myself here because it just so vital to you getting the best out of this book and this exercise in particular: you have to be 100%, absolutely, totally, searingly honest with yourself here. Otherwise, you'll come away from this book thinking it was a waste of time because you didn't get anything out of it and nothing changed.

Yes, I'm putting responsibility for that on you. Watch me now as I lay that at your feet.

When we make that direct comparison, it makes us look at what we'd hoped our lives would be like; our own expectations and dreams. Of course, sometimes as we 'grow up' those dreams change; what we once thought would be important turns out not to be the case. What it doesn't mean though, is that we have to just accept what we have now and not articulate a revised set of desires. I'm not saying that every day will be full of joy, but it should in itself contain at least some of the ingredients of what makes us feel like our time here has meaning. That's only possible if you look at what those ingredients are and then take considered action to put them in place. In short, sticking your head in the sand and trudging on (that doesn't actually work as an image, but you know what I mean!) isn't ever going to bring you what you want. I guess you know that though, otherwise you wouldn't be reading this book.

Whilst we're on the subject of loving life, we ought to talk about your love life. In 'Elimination' we looked at the people you have around you and amongst those was your most intimate relationship(s). I want to come back to that for a moment here because I believe, as women, that's frequently the most crucial relationship that stands between us and our self-worth, which in turns stands between us and our ability to be selfish.

Of course, I don't know where you're at with your love life as you read this book. You could be anywhere on a spectrum from blissfully single through to miserably coupled up; there are lots of permutations, huh?

Whatever your 'relationship status' I'm not here to comment on it or give an opinion about specifics. What I do want to do is just act a little like the 'grit in the oyster'—as I seek to do in all of these areas—to make you think a little; prompt you to take a fresh look. It's like handing you a new pair of glasses that alter how you see the world.

What matters to me is you. What specifically matters to me is that you believe that you matter. When that happens, you'll start thinking, acting and making decisions that come from that solid foundation of knowing that making you a priority is a good thing for you and those around you.

When it comes to our love life, in my experience, this is where women tend to lower their standards. We accept less in terms of how we should be treated and we tolerate more of what we shouldn't. I blame Hollywood. That's not entirely accurate because that's a place and that can't be responsible. What I mean is that I blame the movies that come out of Hollywood, or anywhere really. I blame films that present this idea that having a relationship is all that matters. We all love a bit of romance, of course, but any real relationship that has it's 'happily ever after' that I know of has usually come from effort, some bumps along the road and because there is mutuality of respect that comes with equality and partnership.

In the case of intimate relationships, it can be where we are most afraid of stating our needs. The desire to have something with someone seems to override our usual sensibilities in terms of what we deem to be acceptable behaviour from another person. It comes back to this idea of belonging, to the fear of 'loss' of that connection; this being one of the most important connections in our lives.

My point? We need to accept the right relationships only. This should be the case in any part of our lives, but most especially when it comes to the person we spend most of our time on. Either physically with or thinking about or expending emotional energy upon—you all know the kind of obsessing I'm referring to!

It doesn't help that the world still behaves like being single is a disease. Something to be guarded against. That if we haven't found someone to be with then we're going to end up sad, lonely and with a house overrun by cats. Think Miss Havisham in Dickens' 'Great Expectations'—now there was a woman who suffered heartbreak and never recovered from it. OK, so perhaps it's not just Hollywood and films that are to blame.

Let's remember that there are lots of single people who are really happy; their lives are full, uncomplicated and they didn't have to spend a pandemic lockdown in close proximity to someone whose personal habits drove them insane! There are lots of very unhappy people in relationships. In fact, moaning about one's other half is practically a national pastime. Make that a global pastime! It's all about perspective and that's something we get to choose.

That's what I want you to get here. I want to encourage you to take some time out to really think about that closest relationship. What advice would you give to a best friend if they were in your situation? What would you say to your younger self? I want you to be your own best adviser about this stuff. Accept only the best for you. Don't make excuses for others' behaviour either.

A couple more of points about having a life you love.

"If you build it, he will come," is a line from the 1989 film 'Field of Dreams'. There's not any connection between that film and anything I want to say here, other than that line is true in life. It doesn't have to be a 'he'; it can be a 'she' or a 'they'. It can be friends, family or lovers. The purpose of me sharing the quote is that is how we should look at our lives.

Build the life you want. Fill it with things you love. Be passionate about what you do. Be selective about how you spend your time and money. Be thoughtful about who you have around you. When you do all those things, you'll love your life. You'll fall in love who you are in that life (but more of that later in the second 'S' element...). That's not to say that there won't be dark days or tough times, but as an umbrella feeling, your life will be one that lights you up from inside. You'll shine. When you shine, the right people—your kind of people—will be attracted to that light. Your vibe attracts your tribe. If you're looking for love, for a relationship—the right relationship—whether you're currently single or with someone, then stop looking. Start instead to build that life. The rest will come. It will be drawn to you.

My parting words are about heartbreak. I really hope it's not something you've been through, but I'm guessing for most of you reading this you probably will have. It's kind of a rite of passage; part of growing up. Sadly. For anyone who has read my book, 'All The Twats I Met Along The Way', you'll know I've been through it—I think the title might be a hint!

The reason that I want to highlight heartbreak in particular is that it can be a place where we do ourselves harm. How we handle it, what we tell ourselves when it happens to us, how society responds (or doesn't) when we go through it. If it has happened to you, I think you'll know what I mean. If you're going through it right now - I'm sorry. Deeply. I understand your pain and that it's physical not just emotional. Know that you're not alone. Know that it does heal, even if right now it feels like it won't. There are things you can do to ease the process so that it stops being so hard on you. Access my top tips for 'How to handle heartbreak' at www.carolynhobdey. com. You'll find helpful advice on ways to get through it for you or someone you're supporting at a difficult time. Just remember: this too will pass.

## L is for Loving life
## Activity

*How to build a life you love*

Answer the following three questions in detail about your life as it is today.

- When you look around you, what do you see?

- Tune in to the sounds: what can you hear?

- How do you feel about this life?

Now take a moment to visualise the life you want and answer the same three questions again.

Conduct a comparison of your two outputs.

For a document to complete this activity as well as further **loving life** resources, find them at: www.carolynhobdey.com/RedefiningSELFISH/Resources

*S.E.L.F.I.S.H*

*F is for Failure*

What is it that happens to our feelings about failure as we grow up? When we're toddlers who are learning to walk, failure is celebrated by those around us: the fact we tried, how far we got, the slightest improvement, the encouragement to get up and try again. Yet, somewhere along the line we learn to fear it; we learn to see it as something to be avoided at all costs. How and when does that change occur?

The honest answer is that I have no idea! It merely struck me how we move from the positive to the negative as far as failure is concerned. I think that must happen fairly early on our lives. Why? Because much of that dialogue is in our heads—back to the stories we tell ourselves about ourselves—and I think that dialogue about all sorts of things gets formed in our childhoods. As I said earlier, our values set and beliefs system are usually in place around the age of seven.

When it comes to most things, but in respect of failure

particularly, there will usually have been something that occurred that left an imprint; a negative fear of getting it wrong. Of not being perfect. That 'thing' will be a sense of shame/embarrassment/ridicule/loss.

It may have happened at home, at school or a leisure activity. Wherever it occurs, we hold on to those experiences as part of our warning mechanism in the future. They alert us to danger, which is why the 'fear' is placed in our bodies as a reminder and becomes a physiological response that we have to work hard to control.

Failure is one of the mindsets that I'd like us to look at shifting as part of our efforts to be kinder to ourselves. This is because we all fail, but somehow, we just don't view it as a very common occurrence that we should be comfortable with as a result.

I spent years (it feels like a lifetime) being a perfectionist. My first ever line manager—a wonderful, wise man—said to me when I was in my early twenties: "You don't know how to do just enough, do you?". He was absolutely right. I couldn't conceive of what that even looked like. How did you know what 'just enough' was? Why wouldn't you want to do your best at everything? Not giving your all seemed unthinkable. Alien.

I learnt the hard way—mentally and physically—the damage that trying to give 100% to everything can have. It exhausted me and numerous people around me, I'm ashamed to say. I was so driven to get things 'right', to not fail, to not fall short, to try and be the best (not competitively against others I might add, but so as not to disappoint myself) that I ran the risk on several occasions of running myself into the ground. One such situation of sustained attack on my personal reserves has left an imprint on my health that still rears itself today when I get stressed. We forget that our bodies don't always let us forget.

Despite that, I still have to fight that 'perfect' demon sometimes; to remind myself when enough is enough. Sometimes, we won't be 'finished', but we have to know when it is time to stop.

Perfectionism is a fear of failure, so that's one of the behaviours we need to commit to giving up. No-one is perfect. In our social media world we have to understand the difference between 'reel' and 'real'. That is, the former being the edited highlights of someone's life—the parts they want to show you—with the latter being the truth of what is undoubtedly a very imperfect life. Because all of our lives are that. We're fallible. We drop stuff. We trip over: actually and metaphorically.

I'm not saying that every mistake has to be played out in a public arena because nothing has to be played out in public if we choose for it not to be—that should be our right unless we're courting publicity—but how we make failure OK is not to judge, criticise, shame and/or call it out when someone else's shortcomings come to our attention. Honestly, we only behave that way because their failure taps into a fear inside of us. What we should spend our time doing is understanding what that fear is. Is it because if we tried, we're afraid that we'd fail too? Does their failure remind us of something we failed at and it evokes a strong, negative emotional reaction? Is that person trying to do something that we'd like to do, but we didn't have the courage to try, so dragging them down makes us feel better about our inability to step up?

I get that none of those things makes us sound great and it might be hard to admit that we could do them, but we're all human and it's the kind of negative behaviour we can easily get drawn into when we're not feeling good about ourselves. It's another reason why we need to shift our mindset towards positive self-talk. Doing our own thing, trying some stuff, setting ourselves up with aims for what we want to get out of life. . . they all help. This way, whatever someone else is doing becomes so much less important to us, but we're also more inclined to celebrate and support them for at least trying to do something; we're doing things too and would welcome that same encouragement. It stops being about competition or comparison and starts being about collaboration.

I'd like us to look instead at adopting a 'freedom to fail' attitude. One where we make it OK to mess up. An attitude that enables us to hold our hands up when we make a mistake, apologise when we need to (but ONLY when we need to! I have traditionally been the Queen of 'Sorry, sorry, sorry') and then—here's the magic ladies—move on. Yes, you heard me. Put down that 'failure', step over it and start walking away from it. Don't look back. Don't go back. Don't pick it back up again. Definitely don't beat yourself with it.

Yes, take the lesson from it. Hold onto the memory of what happened. The trick is though: use that for good. Find the positive in the horror/shame/embarrassment that you felt in the moment and use that emotion to better you rather than letting the negative emotion that you felt at the time of the incident stay with you. It's a subtle but marked difference. Each time we take something bad and turn it into something good we're reinforcing that positive mindset; the one that is productive rather than destructive.

If you struggle to do this for you, start by making a conscious effort to find the positives in the failures of friends/family/colleagues. Chances are that you already do and it's only *you* that you're hard on when mistakes occur. I say this as the voice of experience here. I could see the 'sunny side' for everyone else and all I did was beat myself up for being an 'idiot' when I perceived I had fallen short. It's mad, isn't it? Yet, when you focus on finding the upside to others' failures, you'll soon start to see the benefits to your thought processes about your own mistakes. Ask yourself: what did I learn from this experience? Why was it good for me to have gone through this? How did I grow as a result? What will I do differently next time/in a similar situation?

Remember: it's not how you fall down that matters, it's how you get back up that counts. And there's the thing. How we handle our setbacks is the legacy we leave on others. Whilst I stand by my assertion that we worry about what people think about us, when in reality most of them aren't actually watching, there will be a small number of people around us who either consciously or subconsciously learn from the way in which we handle failure. How we deal with it teaches them. For most of you that will be the children or young people in your life: whether your own children or in your extended family, those who you coach/teach or the children of friends. They are particularly susceptible to absorbing our attitudes to failure. If you lead or manage people at work, they will be watching too.

That's what I want you to think about here. Who is it that you want to be a positive role model for when it comes to failure? Who do you know it's important to show that you practice what you preach when mistakes happen? When we find some accountability outside of ourselves, evidence shows that we are much more likely to stick at something. Who can you be accountable to with your failure mindset that will hold you to making sure that your mindset is positive? You don't have to tell them. You just have to tell you. When you fail, imagine they are there with you and can watch your actions, hear your words and—most importantly of all—can read your mind. I guarantee it will change your approach. It will pull you up short.

My final point on failure is what I call 'falling off the wagon'. What do I mean by this? It's that thing we're inclined to do when we fail. We have that tendency to behave like a petulant child. You know the thing. . . 'Well that's it, it's all ruined!' and you metaphorically throw your toy on the floor/tear up the painting you were doing/storm off the playing field. Whatever the childhood scenario, you get my drift. When 1% doesn't go as we want, we trash the other 99% and throw in the towel. What do I mean in the adult world? You eat a doughnut when you're on a diet so the diet goes 'out the window' and you gorge on everything in sight. You have a bad five minutes at 7am and decide that this is 'a bad day'. The taxi fails to show and your entire evening out 'is ruined'. Really?!

We've all done it at some time. Whether the tantrum shows itself overtly or it just goes on in our minds, we've all lived up to the saying: 'throwing the baby out with the bathwater.'

Why? It's usually fear of failure. It's the excuse to stop trying when something gets difficult. It's our 'out' of something we don't really want to do. We use it as evidence that we're useless/hopeless/ridiculous—insert whatever word goes on in your head—and as the reason we should quit.

So here's the thing. One bad five minutes doesn't dictate

or cancel out the other 1,435 potentially 'good' minutes in a day. Honestly. I'm not making that up. There isn't actually a law that says that it does. You can choose—yes you, ridiculous, useless, failing you—can decide that the rest of that day can be good. That one doughnut? It doesn't mark the end of the diet. Even if you ate the other five doughnuts in the packet. . . you can just draw a line under it, get back on the diet 'wagon' and keep going. Better still, you can learn what the trigger was for allowing yourself to eat all the doughnuts and use that knowledge to put some things in place to prevent it happening again. See?! A positive change in mindset. Who knew?!

You get my point. Our failures do not define our day/our lives/us. They can only do that if we give them disproportionate power over us. Let's stop that. Time to give it up.

How?

Choose.

Choose your attitude to your mistakes.

Choose how you move on from failure.

Choose to lay your imperfections in any day to rest at night as you go to bed and get up the next without them weighing you down.

It's time we all allowed ourselves to feel lighter.

> *"Every day the clock resets.*
> *Your wins don't matter.*
> *Your failures don't matter.*
> *Don't stress on what was, fight for what could be."*
> - Sean Higgins

## F is for Failure
## Activity

*How to reframe failure*

Write down something that you failed at recently.

Now, identify all the positives that could come from it, what lessons you've learnt and how you're going to approach the same situation differently in the future.

For a document to complete this activity as well as further **failure** resources, find them at: www.carolynhobdey.com/ RedefiningSELFISH/Resources

# S.E.L.F.I.S.H

## I is for Identity

*"It's really difficult to love someone that you don't know."*
-Sara Kuburic-

After my life had been razed to the ground, one of the things I discovered was that I didn't know who I was. I'd been so malleable that I'd become what everyone else needed me to be. Very little of me was for me. I'd lost sight of what I stood for.

I had a lot of 'labels'. Identities and personas I had taken on: partner, stepmother, friend, daughter, employee, sister, boss, ex-wife, client, auntie, leader. None of these were bad things to be known as, indeed many of them were roles I loved and was honoured to hold, but they were all external to me; they were about pleasing everyone else. My confidence in what I stood for had been severely dented in my last relationship without doubt, but in many ways it—I—had been eroded over a much longer period of time. I felt like I was a collection of everyone else's disparate parts of me. What sat at the core of who I was appeared to be blurred. Foggy, distant, diminished.

Don't get me wrong, I wasn't some kind of weak-willed, pathetic, beige character; in many ways I was quite the opposite of that. Yet, even that vibrancy appeared like it just got me into 'trouble'; that in many areas—especially via the males in my life—they just thought I ought to tone it down. Somewhere that light still shone, but it had been dimmed to such an extent in order to 'fit in' with what others wanted that it seemed like it had been all but extinguished.

It took time for me to really see that. I think what took the time was for me to realise that I could have that shining core. That I deserved to have a significant part of me that was about me. That I was entitled to be 'Carolyn' before I was any of those other things to other people. That what that would mean was that I'd possess a strength and certainty of 'self' that would actually better serve the people around me.

I learnt that those who were positive in my life loved it when I shone; in whatever form that took for me to be happy. Those that were toxic? Well, that light blinded them so greatly that they usually left of their own accord!

That's why the 'I' in the S.E.L.F.I.S.H. model stands for 'Identity'. We have to know who WE are before we can support those we care about with being who THEY are. Why? Because who wants to dampen down others out of a fear founded within our own uncertainty? We can only help others shine when first we shine. Especially those we are role models for: our families, our children, the people we lead.

So, do you know who you are? Can you describe yourself

without reference to the roles you play for others and the labels that get placed upon you?

Yes, those things might make up who you are, but you first have to be 'enough' without them. You need to stand for what you stand for, then add those parts; wear them like layers of clothes that you take on and off a body that is already fully formed.

When was the last time you really spent time considering who you are? In our lives full of busy-ness, it's not something we usually have head space for, is it? We think we sort of know who we are and then we just crack on with doing stuff and meeting the numerous demands of daily life.

Let's press pause on all of that then for a bit. Once again, we're going to focus on you. I know—sometimes this process feels really uncomfortable, doesn't it? Putting you first, talking about you—eek! Well, time to get over yourself on that front! Repeat after me (out loud) please:

I. AM. IMPORTANT.

Not so hard, was it? Actually, do that every day for a month and see what happens. Set an alarm on your phone to remind yourself to do it (although I'd suggest not to do it in a meeting or randomly on public transport—although you'd probably get a whole seat to yourself if you did!).

Time to take a look at who you are.

Start with the easy stuff and that which will still be at the top of your mind, despite what I've said! Begin by writing down all the labels and roles you have (mother, manager, environmentalist, etc.) so that we get those out of the way.

Done? There's probably lots of them, aren't there? All that stuff you do for others. It makes you a wonderful human being, but it doesn't make you. . . *you*.

Now let's write down all the things you'd say about yourself. I want you to write a long list first, of whatever comes into your head about who you are: words/phrases you'd say about yourself if asked or just inside your own head. I especially want you to get out the ones in your own head—that self-talk is vital to expose (don't worry, you're only exposing it to you, not to anyone else). Don't write what you *want* to be said about you. Write what is *actually* said in your head.

The next thing I want you to do is to take each of those things that you wrote to describe yourself and place them into two columns as follows:

- Positive things about me.
- Negative things about me.

Then look at the two lists and compare the number of items in each column. I'm not going to ask you to do anything with that other than 'notice' it because you'll know yourself what it means/how it feels if one column has more items in it than the other. Based on everything you've read in this book so far, I hope that I don't need to ask you to do anything other than compare and notice. And have a think about it.

Sorry, did I sound a bit like your mother sending you to your room to reflect on your behaviour and think about what you've done? That wasn't intentional. Although quite amusing. . . perhaps.

Next, I want you to write down the things that other people would say about you. Think across all the areas of your life and all the different people you come into contact with. The list can be positive or negative things that they'd say. I want you to dig deep on all those pieces of feedback, things that stung, throw-away comments, compliments that you probably chose to ignore... Again, once you've brain-stormed them all, place them into 'Positive' and 'Negative' columns.

As before, take a good look at the two lists. How many and what kind of things have you written? Compare these lists to the ones you wrote about you. Think about the similarities and differences. Ask yourself: how do I talk to myself versus how others speak about me? What is good and bad about that? How do all these lists make me feel as I look through them?

I'm deliberately not making any judgements or comments here. I don't know what might be on your lists or how long each one might be; that's between you and the lists. I just want you to complete the exercise and take a step back to look at what it tells you about how *you* speak to *you* and what others say. Just taking a moment to 'see' it all is what counts.

What I observed in my life is that I spent a lot of time living up to other people's expectations. Their 'shoulds' about what I ought to do, who I should be, what they thought I should do. Lots of layers were placed upon me until I was buckling under the weight of it all. Don't get me wrong, there were plenty of expectations I placed upon me too, but nearly all of it came from a place of pleasing everyone else.

I want you to know that you don't have to do that. You might argue with me about that because we often feel like we have no choice, but usually we have plenty of choice; it's just that some of those choices might be a bit tricky to implement. Make sure you are clear about the difference between those things in your life. Don't confuse 'that's quite hard to do' with 'no choice' because that is, in reality, just an excuse.

I cannot tell you what your identity should be. That's for you to determine. It's whatever rings true to you and your values set. Therefore, where we're going to conclude this section of the model is by writing down what you want to stand for. This is about how you're going to define yourself. Yes, it's about what you want others to say about you, but that's based on you being your authentic self and showing up as that person in yours and others' lives so that what they have to say about you is exactly what you'd want them to say because it is in line with what you'd say about you.

When we state 'out loud' to ourselves what we stand for and who we are going to be, it brings it to life. When it's written down it becomes like a reference document for us—something that we can go back to in order to ensure that we maintain the standard we set, to boost us on a difficult day and remind ourselves to have the courage of our convictions in the face of opposition.

That's what you're going to do as the final activity in this section. You're going to write a statement, a commitment if you like, about who you're going to be going forward. One that states what you will and won't accept in your life. To do that, here are some prompts and questions to get you started. If you want a template to follow, you can find one on my website: www.carolynhobdey.com/RedefiningSELFISH/Resources.

**The Character Commitment: how to set the standard for who you are**

Start with this phrase: 'From today I am going to be a person who. . .'

Then think about the following:

- What values do you most want to exhibit in your day-to-day life? What do you want to be known for/ people to say about their experience of you?
- What behavioural standards are you going to set for yourself? What will you accept? What won't you accept from you?
- What treatment and behaviours will you expect from others? What won't you tolerate? How will you handle bad/toxic behaviours to ensure you remain true to your standards?
- How do you want people to feel when they have interacted with you? What energy do you want to live within and exude to other people?

This statement doesn't have to be a literary masterpiece. It doesn't matter how long or short it is. What it does have to be is from the heart. It is a *standard* that you are setting for yourself and your life. It is about YOU being front and centre of saying, 'this is who I am, how I expect to treat others and be treated'. It's all about bringing the S.E.L.F.I.S.H. model to life. Write it. Step away from it for a while. Let it settle. Read the remainder of the book. Come back and review it. Amend if necessary. You can amend it as much as you like in the weeks, months and years ahead. Promise me one thing though: never amend it to lower your standards. That I won't accept.

Once you've written your current, best version of your commitment, I want you to put this statement somewhere that you can easily access it. Email it to yourself. Save it onto your phone. If you have a friend that you trust, share it with them. Ask them to hold you to account to remain true to it, especially with regards to the standards of how you treat yourself and what you'll accept with regards to others' treatment of you; this is particularly important if you're committed to being S.E.L.F.I.S.H.

**I is for Identity**
**Activity**

*How to reclaim your identity*

List out all the 'role' labels you (or others) apply to yourself.

Next write down all the things you'd say about you that don't involve those labels—the things that are about your identity.

For a document to complete this activity as well as further **identity** resources, find them at: www.carolynhobdey.com/RedefiningSELFISH/Resources

## S is for Sexiness

Did you cringe when you saw this one?

For similar reasons that we discussed right at the start of this book, we're conditioned to believe that thinking of ourselves as 'sexy' is an act of conceitedness that is actively discouraged in females. Add to that the messages we get from society that by presenting our sexual side to the world it makes us 'fair game' for ridicule and, worse still, that it means we're 'up for it' or 'asking for it' with anyone that wants to take it from us whether we consent or not. . .

I hate to sound like some bra-burning, tub-thumping, anti-male feminist (I could write a whole other book about how the meaning of feminism has been taken and contorted from something positive to negative, but I digress. . .) because I am none of those things. I just find it sad that a woman's feminine, sexual side cannot be displayed without it being exploited and turned on her like a weapon. Because here's a thing. . . wait for it. . . you can be both feminine/sexy AND smart. I know! Who knew?! There isn't actually any need to 'play dumb' in order to make ourselves appear more attractive. Similarly, there's no requirement to pretend to be a-sexual in order to be considered intelligent. Femininity and geeky can go hand in hand; it is possible to flutter your eyelashes and do calculus AT THE SAME TIME! Fact!

On a serious note though, our femininity is a fundamental part of who we are; it should be celebrated. First and foremost, it should be celebrated by us. There are characteristics associated with 'female traits' that are incredibly positive and we should emphasise these to use them for good; they should not be belittled or qualities that we feel we should mask. In contrast, they shouldn't be weaponised by us against men either. Personally, I find it totally unhelpful to the improvement of the perception of females when you find women 'shouting' at men over social media. No argument ever got won—and no-one was ever persuaded to change their mind—when being yelled at. Calm discussion with the intention of creating understanding only please, ladies. Thank you.

Give me a moment to climb down off my soap box. . .

There. That's better. Back to the topic at hand.

When I talk about 'sexiness' here, I mean it holistically. For me it is a combination of the following things:

- Confidence: how we feel as much as in how we look.
- Sassiness: it being OK to rock a bit of (positive) attitude.
- Regarding our feminine traits as assets.
- Having the courage to own our patch of the world.
- Standing tall/not apologising for being a woman.

What I absolutely do <u>not</u> mean is:

- Pitting men and women against each other.
- Being overly, uncomfortably sexual.
- The negative, aggressive connotations that 'feminism' has become associated with (I'd encourage you to look up the definition of feminism as it was not intended to be this way).
- Pretending to be something you're not.

Now that we've got that cleared up, let's take a look at how we can bring sexy back (thank you Mr Timberlake) without wanting to curl up in a ball whilst waiting for the ground to swallow us up with embarrassment.

OK, it's time to chat confidence.

What a topic this is. . . Our relationship with confidence is a mixed-up thing, is it not? Too much confidence and we risk getting labelled, amongst other things, as:

- Aggressive (when you're just being assertive).
- Emotional (I particularly hate the way this is used to shut women down/dismiss them).
- Masculine (when a woman chooses to behave like a man to get on).
- Up herself (oh, so I'm not allowed to value myself?).
- Dislikeable (so the only way I can be liked is to be meek and mild?).

Unfortunately, the list could go on and on. . .

By contrast, too little overt confidence and women get characterised as:

- Weak.
- Submissive.
- Plain.
- Unable/unsuitable to lead.
- Unambitious.
- Not to be taken seriously.

There's no surprise that we don't know which way to turn!

It is interesting to make a comparison with the (positive) way that a confident man gets described. Forgive me, I do keep coming back to the male/female thing, but when it comes to confidence and sexuality there are, undeniably, different standards by which the male and female sexes are judged. That is, women are judged and men less so. That's not to say it is the fault of 'all men'. Nor am I saying that women are blameless; there are many that don't aid the cause with the worst, in my experience, being those that over-exaggerate masculine behaviours in the workplace.

We know that we might need to tread a fine line with how our confidence manifests itself. We're not going to 'fix' the whole of society or how different cultures perceive women, but we can address what confidence means to us as individuals. Often, behaviours (in women) that get interpreted as 'lacking confidence' don't necessarily mean they are, internally, unconfident.

However, I do meet so many people, with more being female (but not exclusively) who bemoan their lack of confidence. We need to start with our perception of what confidence is. To do this, I want to talk about what it isn't.

Confidence isn't some kind of mythical gift that is bestowed upon us; it's not presented to us externally by someone else. Confidence is not something that we are either blessed with or not. I'm here to tell you that it simply isn't true that if you don't 'have' confidence that this situation cannot change. It can. It starts with understanding where confidence comes from. I saw a formula recently that is useful to share here because it brings together elements of a number of points I've written about already in this book:

$$Congruence + Competence + Connection = Confidence$$
-Lewis Howes-

I love this formula. It captured the things I bang on about all the time! Let's break it down so that it's clear how you can achieve confidence by adopting the mindsets and undertaking the activities that I advocate all the time to my clients (and in this book).

Congruence is all about knowing who you are and being true to that person. When we live and behave in a way that isn't really 'us'—because of others' expectations, our own or because we don't articulate what we really want out of life—it creates a discomfort in us that means we are incongruent with who we really are. It's what I mean about living a lie. The reality is that the person to whom we're lying most is ourselves.

This is why I made one of the elements of this model about Identity: knowing who you are and living in accordance with that. This allows you to live as your authentic self more effectively. Congruence comes from this, which means you have the ability to increase your confidence by spending time determining the person you want to be.

Competence is about knowing what your capabilities are so that you can believe in them. It's why I asked you to examine the stories you tell yourself, how you 'measure' yourself, the judgements you place upon yourself; it's why I wanted you to look at how you approach failure. By looking at the skills you have, and assessing the experiences you've been through, you can take away from those all the numerous capabilities you already possess; you can then transfer those to deal with either a current or future situation. Having assuredness in your competence gives you confidence. The great thing with competence is that you're *always* building upon it (even if you don't realise it) and you can consciously do so. Yet another way that you can control the increase in your confidence.

The relationships we have with others—friends, family, colleagues, neighbours—are vital to us. Having positive connections with others is part of what brings quality to our life, more so than anything else in fact. It also relates to what we looked at in the Elimination element: minimising or removing the people that potentially interfere with you being who you are. Actively managing those relationships helps us to have the right connections, not just any connections, because the right ones involve trust and being able to rely on someone when times are tough. If the era of the global pandemic has taught us anything, it's how much we need those people to help us get through the darkest moments. We can change those relationships in our lives—increase the positive ones, reduce the negative ones—so once again our ability to improve our confidence is within our control.

Suddenly, being more confident doesn't seem so hard, does it? It's never about 'you just need to be more confident'. I hate it when people say that. It makes me want to say: "Oh my word, there I was all this time not knowing 'the answer', thank you for showing me the light. Give me a minute and I'll just flick on the 'confidence' switch and fire that up!". Doh!

Yet, if you work on being you. If you remind yourself of all the skills and abilities you already have (which you can keep accumulating just by going about your day-to-day life). If you surround yourself with people who treat you in line with your standard and don't tolerate those that don't. Your confidence will naturally bloom.

All of this leads into the other things I listed at the start of this section as to what 'sexiness' means. That positive attitude (sassiness), which we naturally exude when we are just a bit more self-assured; it's attractive. I mean 'attractive' in its widest sense, not just in an intimate relationship way. Friends, colleagues, new people we meet will all be more drawn to you when you're positive—it gives you a presence that others like. This then gives you that feeling of standing tall on your own patch of the world. However 'small' you might feel that patch is in relation to the whole world out there, remember that there is no greater legacy than the imprint we leave on those we come into contact with. Make it a positive one.

Then add to that pride in your femininity. Women—and those with female traits—are more balanced across both Intelligence Quotient (IQ) and Emotional Intelligence (EQ) with the latter being 'a central quality for effective leadership' (source: T. Chamorro-Premuzic). This means that females are less likely to create toxic workplace cultures and more likely to generate greater engagement in employees.

Outside of the workplace this translates to a more enhanced ability to sense how others are feeling and to respond positively to their needs. In addition, higher EQ equates to an improved ability to recover from setbacks, greater self-control and enhanced self-awareness (source: T. Chamorro-Premuzic). Like, what's not to love about all of that?! We should be celebrating our femaleness because it's awesome! Just stop pointing at every other woman you know and saying she has those qualities and start seeing them in you too.

With all that going for you, you have every reason to feel 'sexy'.

Before I sign off from this section, I just want to say a few words here about the menopause. Now, you might be at a stage in life where this seems quite far off and not of interest. I would disagree on two fronts:

1.  I discovered at 32 years old that I had already been through the menopause and when I worked it back realised it started in my early twenties, maybe even earlier (again, more about that in my book, 'All The Twats I Met Along The Way').
2.  Our ignorance/lack of discussion about the menopause as women is a concern and it's actually never too early to educate yourself about it—you'll go through it, other women in your life will go through it—so get clued up now.

Similarly, you may already be out the other side of the

menopause and think this part isn't for you. I'd argue it is for you because our understanding can still be developed for our own benefit and in support of others.

For many women, when they reach the menopause (at whatever age, but the average age is 51 years old so let's use that as a rule-of-thumb here), a number of things may happen. After all, there are about 34 different symptoms associated with the menopause so given that you could have any combination of them and each one to varying degrees it's not surprising we're confused by it! Common amongst women's experiences are a loss of libido and a sense at that stage in their life of becoming 'invisible' (some of the impacts of the menopause sometimes mean we want to, so it's a double-edged sword this one!).

I get, therefore, that I might be asking you to stand tall and embrace your sexiness at a time you feel anything but. I want to acknowledge that. I didn't know what it was when it was happening to me, but I understand it with the benefit of hindsight (and a proper medical diagnosis, finally).

The menopause is, not for all but for many, tough. Physically and emotionally it's a challenge; the lack of understanding and support that a lot of women experience makes this harder still. It is common for women to present at the GP (even female doctors) with menopause symptoms and come away instead with antidepressants and feelings of confusion or embarrassment.

And here I am suggesting you get your 'sass' on and rock some attitude. I know it's not that easy. I know it's harder still if your hormones are topsy-turvy and the brain-fog means you can't spell 'sexy' let alone feel it.

What I'm here to tell you is: this too will pass. I know I keep saying it, but it's true in life. Whilst we live often in ignorance of the duration of the menopause (end-to-end it can last up to 10 years. Sorry if that revelation is like a sledge hammer), it will not be the same experience throughout it and it WILL END.

What I want to encourage you to do is to use the techniques and strategies I suggest in this book to aim to keep confidence levels up as much as possible whilst you're going through the menopause. Confidence is reported to dip massively during menopause with a high proportion of very smart, capable women quitting their jobs because symptoms feel unmanageable and unsupported in the workplace.

I also want you to rock your sass on the good days. I want you to know that your life, your femininity and your sex-appeal are not over because of this life event. All of it is still there and it will come back to you; perhaps with some medical intervention (if that's right for you), a bit of encouragement from you and by maintaining some selfishness in the meantime.

Finally, as a plea, if you don't feel like you're getting the medical support you need during the menopause, please keep going back to your GP or ask to see someone else. Switch GP surgeries if need be. Don't apologise for having these symptoms. Don't apologise for saying: "This is still an issue and I need more help". Ask your friends about their experiences of the menopause (we still need to get better at that) and whether they have a referral to a doctor with whom they had a good outcome and felt heard.

Right, now it's time for a bit of 'Sexiness' activity before the final element of Redefining S.E.L.F.I.S.H.

## S is for Sexiness
## Activity

*How to live in alignment with your standards*

Go back and remind yourself of the words in your Character Commitment.

Write down three ways in which you could immediately live in a more congruent way with who you are and who you intend to be—starting today!

For a document to complete this activity as well as further **sexiness** resources, find them at: www.carolynhobdey.com/ RedefiningSELFISH/Resources

# *S.E.L.F.I.S.H.*

## *H is for Help*

I've made the 'H' of my model about Help because when we are low in self-worth, far down on our list of priorities, giving all we can to the care and support of others, we frequently forget that we need help too. Worse still is when we don't think we're deserving of it. That's why I'm putting it here.

Yet, don't you find we have a really warped relationship with the concept of asking for help?

It's as if it's something to be ashamed of and avoided. That's because asking for help makes us feel vulnerable. But ask yourself:

How did I feel the last time someone I cared about asked me for help?

Unless they are one of those people who always takes without giving (in which case, please go back and re-read the section on 'Elimination' because I think you might have someone you need to remove or minimise in your life!), then the chances are that you felt. . . honoured, special, privileged, good about yourself, trusted, respected. . .

When someone asks us for help, they're saying to us: you have something that I value.

Invariably, that makes us feel good, doesn't it? It's a boost to our ego. We get a warm, fuzzy feeling. It's pleasant. It makes us want to help them. We're getting something out of it in return.

Asking for help is a reciprocal act of kindness. With the reality being that no-one succeeds by themselves, so we need to help each other.

It begs the question: why do we find it so hard to ask for help when its impact on others can be so positive?

I want to leave that there for a moment for you to think about. . .

I'm hoping that has shifted your mindset about asking for help a little already; that it's made it feel like it's not such a bad thing. Let's keep going, though, as I'm certain there's more work for me to do to convince you.

Maybe to help you (see what I did there?) to get your head around the idea of asking for help, we should look at the technique required. Would that make you feel more at ease about it?

The first thing is to accept that asking for help is in fact a skill that we need to cultivate; that way we get more comfortable with doing it. One of my favourite concepts is one that I learnt a while ago from watching Heidi Grant's TED Talk in 2019. She spoke about the 'Illusion of Transparency'. That is, that our thoughts and needs are obvious to others. What this means in relation to asking for help is that we don't. We wait for others to offer because we think that they will just 'know' that we need help. You can anticipate what happens next. . . they don't see our need; they don't offer help and we get upset that they are ignoring our needs. Then what happens? Oh yes, we start telling ourselves stories about how we don't matter, nobody cares, we're not important and don't deserve their help. . . Please do feel free to correct me if I'm wrong!

The big lesson here is that we need to be prepared to actually ask for the help we need, rather than wait for the offer. If we're going to ask, we'll want to be successful at it; securing a 'yes' is our ideal outcome, right?

Here are some tips, courtesy of Heidi Grant, for improving your chances of success:

- **Be specific about what help you want and why.** This is because those you're asking will need to know if they are able to help you or not. People want to be successful with the help they give, so enabling them to make that assessment clearly will be more likely to secure a 'yes'.
- **Avoid prefacing it with disclaimers, apologies or bribes.** These all make the other person feel uncomfortable before you've even got to the request. Don't incentivise friends and co-workers to help you; this makes it become a transaction and not a relationship (and easier for them to say 'no').
- **Do not ask for help over email or text (mostly).** These methods are impersonal—even if it feels less awkward for you—and much more likely (30% more!)

to get a 'no'. The human touch is much the better way for both parties.

- **If someone agrees to help and does so, then follow up afterwards.** Thank them and tell them HOW it helped you. Knowing that your help landed well is great for the helper (and they will probably help you again!).

Now that you're going to be a Ninja at asking for help, we have to tackle the other part of our difficulty with this concept: accepting help.

If you've actually asked for help then you are probably already in the mindset of accepting it if you've received a 'yes' to your request. Although I don't take that as a given; I've been guilty of getting part way through the help being given, becoming uncomfortable and doing the verbal or physical communication of 'thank you, that's enough now'. So make sure if you've asked for help you let the helper finish providing what you asked for.

If you've not asked for help and it's offered, then we need to rehearse how to respond so that our needs get met. Here are some scenarios and options:

## A. Help gets offered and it's the help you need.

Say 'yes' for goodness sake! 'Thank you, that would be awesome!' or something similar. I know that sounds simple, patronising even, but it's incredible how often we get an offer of help and we let shame/embarrassment get in the way of accepting it.

I know admitting we need help is an act of vulnerability, but it's exactly that—not to be confused with a weakness. Showing vulnerability is a strength. It says: 'I trust you with this and I'm comfortable to share it'. If someone exploits that vulnerability then you know what I'm going to say. . . Yep, go back and re-read the section on 'Elimination' and make some conscious choices about the role that person plays in your life going forward.

**B. Help gets offered, but it's not the help you need.**
Start with a thank you, obviously, because this person has seen past the 'Illusion of Transparency' after all and recognised that help is needed. Next, you have to articulate what help you actually need. Then, as in the list above, the person is able to assess whether they are the right person to help you or not. If they are, then refer to point 'A' and take it. If they're not, see if they'd still be willing to help you, but by identifying the right person to give the help you need.

**C. Help gets offered, but you're not sure what help you need**
As in point 'B', begin by recognising that someone has seen that you need help; this is a great start for both of you. If that person is already in a place of 'helpfulness', then likelihood is they have some compassion for the signs you're demonstrating of needing help. In which case, use their offer to help you understand what help you need. By talking it through and articulating what the issue is, you'll gain clarity together about how best to move forward. Then you can go to point 'A' if they can help or point 'B' if you need their help to find the right support.

I want to say out loud here that the concept of the 'stiff upper lip' is bollocks. Of course, we need to have strength and resilience, but I'm guessing you've already got that in spades because you've probably been dealing with life, handling stuff and behaving like 'Superwoman' for quite some time now. So your abilities in this area are not in question. Can we agree that?

The 'Help' section is about the fact that you don't need to do this stuff alone. Yes, sometimes you're the only person who can do something or know something, but that doesn't mean that you cannot lean on your support network for emotional support. I'd also like you to question whether you really are the only person that can do something—or is that just a position you *like* to be in. We all want to feel needed and valued, but are you getting that by making yourself indispensable in some way? Be really honest with yourself about that. You cannot moan about not being helped or supported or being the general dogsbody if you've created that situation. Are you helping others to be helpless? If you are, that's not love and care; that's destructive to them and you. Take some time to examine your thoughts and behaviours in this regard. There might be some uncomfortable truths in there. Whilst you're at it, ask yourself why you have that need to be needed by others. What is it that you're not valuing about yourself that means that you need that external validation?

If you find that's the case, then it's even more important that you complete all the activities in this book and I'd encourage you to do the additional ones available on my website too because they will really assist you with cementing some changes in mindset and behaviour. Shifting this relationship with yourself is what Redefining S.E.L.F.I.S.H. is all about.

### H is for Help
### Activity

*How to accept help*

Download from my website the three responses to when help is offered.

Commit them to memory and start using them—immediately!

For a document to complete this activity as well as further **help** resources, find them at: www.carolynhobdey.com/RedefiningSELFISH/Resources

# CHAPTER 5

## *How do you take the first step towards S.E.L.F.I.S.H.?*

When we consider putting ourselves first, especially after a long period of not doing so, and prioritising everyone else, it can feel overwhelming to get started. So much easier to think, 'yeah that's all great, now what's the next thing on my to-do list?'. The answer to *that* is, as we've established already, very unlikely to be anything that's for you.

But what we've looked at here is serious. You cannot carry on feeling this way. You cannot carry on treating yourself this way. You owe it to you. You owe it to those you love to be a role model for self-care and to put yourself in the best shape possible to continue to care for them (without the burnout, weariness and irritation you doubtless feel sometimes!).

You know you need to do something differently, don't you?

Let's look at how you get started so that you don't feel overwhelmed and just go back to doing what you were doing, thinking the way you were thinking before you started this book. I am hoping that just reading this has already changed some of that, but for new habits to replace old habits (both physically and mentally) we have to get consistent for them to stick. We need to make them rituals rather than habits.

When you want to start doing things differently, you need to have a plan. I know that sounds boring and painful, but it's true. None of this will happen by accident. No-one is going to come and wave a magic wand to change your life or your thoughts and feelings. You're going to have to take action to put things in place.

Start with the Character Commitment you wrote earlier. That's where you set out who you want to be, starting immediately. Take out that document. Read it. Put it somewhere you can easily access it. If necessary, read it every day for a month. Why? Because research shows it takes about 28 days to break an old habit and to cement a new one. Reminding yourself about who you intend to be every day is a great way to start stepping into the change you're going to make. Ideally, read that Commitment every morning; get it out whilst you're boiling the kettle for that first cup of tea/coffee or whilst you're cleaning your teeth.

Therein lies the trick.

When you want to develop a new habit/ritual, build it into or onto something you already do. This is known as 'layering' and it's great way to implement changes. Cleaning your teeth is a great one because we do that every day (hopefully at least twice a day) almost without thinking. Whether it's starting the day by reading your Character Commitment or thinking about how you turn negative thoughts about yourself into positive ones each night before you go to bed, doing those things whilst cleaning your teeth means it's not an 'extra task'. It saves you time and the act of cleaning your teeth can be the prompt for you to do whatever the new habit is.

You get the idea. Don't create more things to do, create smart ways of doing things.

And start small. Do what you can manage. Then build upon it. Layer it up. Doing 'something' and sticking to it builds confidence in our progress. Trying to change everything or doing lots of new stuff just means we're likely to fail and give up. If you do 'fail', by the way, please go back to the section on 'Failure' and re-read that element. Pick yourself up and try again. Oh, and be kind to yourself about it.

The other thing that holds us back is procrastination. Distracting ourselves. Dithering. Finding other things to do other than the thing we really need to do.

Stop that. I mean it! Stop.

Procrastination happens because we're anxious about something. To break it, you need to understand what the source of that anxiety is: what's stressing you out? Really? What is it? Knowing what's at the bottom of that anxiety helps to make dealing with it more tangible. It might not take away the anxiety straight away, but it will move it from a general anxiety to a more specific 'worry'. We can tackle something specific, can't we?

Next, do just one thing—however small—to start tackling the thing that's worrying you. There, you've started to deal with it. Feeling better already, I imagine. Now you've started, you can keep going. Either doing that one thing or the next thing that needs to be done to eradicate the thing that's worrying you. And so on. Once again, it's a matter of 'building'. Small, incremental steps.

Dealing with what's making you procrastinate is part of addressing our general fear of change—whether that's a change of attitude or physical changes in our life. When it comes to that fear there are two elements we need to be mindful of:

1. Our fear of the change.
2. Others' fear of our change.

With regards to your own fear, it's about understanding that you may need to lose some things from your life in order to gain new things. Those losses might be labels we've worn, beliefs we've held, situations we've stayed in too long or people that we need to move away from.

It's only natural to be fearful. We're programmed to see danger so that we can respond to it. In overcoming it you have to remember the life and the legacy you've already stated that you want. That person you've said you're going to be. You've written it down. You've committed. And do keep in mind that the loss of things makes room for new/different/better ones. Those better things are on their way as a result of the change you're about to make.

With regards to other people, there will always be those who object/protest/try to guilt-trip you into not doing what *you* want to because they want you to do what *they* want. When you're drawing up your plan to implement the differences you want to make to your life, you need to spend a bit of time thinking about who might object and what they might not like. Think about how those objections might manifest and how you're going to handle them. In some cases you may have to prepare for a conversation either about the change you're going to make or their reaction whilst you're making it. Obviously, you cannot script those conversations, but think about the points you'd want to make—especially about why you're making the change and what it means to you to do some things in a different way.

The road ahead is likely to be a bit bumpy. When we try anything new, we can be a touch inept. We stumble. We have to get up and try again. You're not unique in that. It happens to us all. That doesn't mean you're not still special in your own way though. You are.

And none of us should be naive enough to think that just reading a book will sort us out. This is just the starting line of a new life. A new you. Remember that you're not alone. You're part of the gang now. The S.E.L.F.I.S.H. gang. A group where you are 'good enough'. A group where we're comfortable with our own and each other's imperfections. Sound good?

Never forget that it's OK to need some more help along the way, so come and join us via the website (www.carolynhobdey. com) and we'll walk alongside you for as long as you need us.

That's because my final point with regards being selfish is to identify your allies. Those people who will support, understand, celebrate and hold you to account for doing some things that are all about you. Use them positively to help you to understand the cost of not being selfish.

Because the cost is high. You lose you. You'll not live the life you want in the way you want. You'll not be that role model or leave that legacy.

Surely these are all bigger reasons to feel guilty than a little bit of selfishness. . .

All the documents to support the activities in this book, plus more, are available to download from my website: www.carolynhobdey.com/RedefiningSELFISH/Resources.

For further information about the work I do and to find out how you can be supported on your path to Redefining SELFISH, find them at: www.carolynhobdey.com

# About the Author

Carolyn Hobdey is the author of 'All The Twats I Met Along The Way' and founder of the Redefining SELFISH community. She lived a life of shame and blame so is now passionate about pioneering new ways of thinking to ensure we live without guilt and regrets.

As founder of the transformational change business, MayDey Ltd, and COO of the lifestyle and recruitment company, 15ten15, Carolyn is a regular speaker and media commentator on issues of toxic relationships, self-esteem, women's health (including the menopause), selfishness, narcissism and many other imperative, topical women's issues.

With more than 20 years spent as an award-winning Human Resources professional in some of the world's largest employers, Carolyn earned a seat at the boardroom table leading internationally recognisable brands. En route, she gained a Masters in Lean Operations at Cardiff University where she was the first HR specialist to undertake the course and became the winner of the inaugural Sir Julian Hodge Prize for Logistics, Operations & Manufacturing.

Carolyn lives in Yorkshire, England and enjoys boxing, dancing and socialising with friends.

# Other books by Carolyn Hobdey

## All The Twats I Met Along The Way

What happens when you so deeply believe something you were told as a child that it becomes the driving force behind almost every thought, feeling and action for the rest of your life – until you decide to take complete control and change your life entirely?

For decades, Carolyn Hobdey believed she was 'trouble' and if she wasn't 'nicer' she'd spend her days alone and unloved.

All The Twats I Met Along The Way is the first in Carolyn's 'Twats Trilogy' and tells the tale of crappy boyfriends, sickening sexual encounters, manipulative men, love triangles, unsupportive and unsupported medical diagnoses... and that's just in the first few pages! From porn-addicted boyfriends who go from fitties to owners of 'dad bods,' to car crashes and boob jobs. Marriage to a lover who became more like a brother (and who harboured a secret Carolyn could not have foreseen) and later a relationship with a man and his 'ready-made family' that exposes a damaging case of coercive control and narcissism. Carolyn's story exposes the unrelenting pull of the child-parent relationship – even in adulthood – and all the messiness, self-esteem issues and confusion that can cause.

## De-Twat Your Life!
**(Spring 2022)**

After her life spectacularly imploded on Friday 13th July 2018, Carolyn began the painful process of picking up the pieces following a brush with suicide.

The caving in of everything she'd known - high-powered job,

beautiful home, a long-term relationship and the 'ready-made' family she'd yearned for - compelled her to press the reset button not just on her world, but on herself. Carolyn looked back across her life and had to confront some uncomfortable truths; not least the numerous warning sirens and red flags she'd diligently ignored along the way.

What resulted was a transformation that razed to the ground who she had become, reconnected her with the person she once was and re-established what she wanted to stand for going forward - taking her experiences with her not as millstones, but as stepping stones to a happier future.

'De-Twat Your Life!' charts the challenging and remarkable story of Carolyn's path out of despair and of finding the courage to allow her innate positivity to shine. It's a tale of self-loathing to self-love that anyone who has endured self-doubt will identify with.

Documenting her trials and triumphs as she dug herself out of the darkest hole of her life and embarked on a long-overdue transformation that changed her mind and body, Carolyn shares the breakthrough moments that led her to develop a unique process that is the 'How To' guide for anyone who wants - or is forced - to undergo change in any area of their life.

This is change, not out of a textbook, but learnt from real life.

No longer will you need to flounder in the face of change, 'De-Twat Your Life!' and Carolyn's step-by-step method will ensure you flourish and have a life well-lived.

## Twats at Work!
### (Autumn 2022)

An extensive and illustrious career took Carolyn all the way to the Boardroom in some of the World's largest employers as she became a leader for numerous of our most internationally recognised brands.

Carolyn has worked with many great people. She has also encountered quite a few twats.

'Twats at Work' provides a peak behind the curtain of corporate life and introduces us to the numerous characters she met; from those that asked for a company policy to address an employee's problem body-odour, through the maverick who could only manage by referring to his 'lead-by-numbers' manual and on to the Executive Board that bore an uncanny resemblance to the British comedy 'WIA'.

This book is for anyone who has ever been led. It is especially for those who have ever been led badly.

Carolyn's experience is that there is an awful lot of the latter, so this book is also for anyone who is a leader and wants to learn how they might do that better.

It examines the great leaders with terrible Imposter Syndrome and the terrible imposters who should never have been allowed to lead.

As a senior leader in Human Resources, Carolyn has pretty much seen it all, which is why she's often heard to say: "Common sense isn't all that common".

Read this book to find out why!

**In praise of Carolyn's work:**

*"All The Twats I Met Along The Way is Carolyn Hobdey's story that a million and one women are going to resonate with, laugh along with, sigh and cry with. It's a story of growing up, moving on, falling down and getting back up again. Transformation and acceptance, strength and resilience."*
**Helen Lewis, Literally PR**

*"By turns funny, incisive and painful, Hobdey's unflinchingly honest account of a series of disastrous relationships will resonate with every woman who has loved unwisely."*
**Frances Hardy, The Daily Mail**

# Would you like to work with Carolyn Hobdey?

So, you've read the book... what next?

Becoming SELFISH won't happen like flicking a switch. It won't occur in one big bang. Changing your mindset and behaviours requires new habits; it takes many small actions, done consistently.

You're not alone. I'm here to walk with you as you continue your journey to Redefining S.E.L.F.I.S.H.

Visit www.carolynhobdey.com to work with Carolyn.

## Group session:
## Single S.E.L.F.I.S.H. element
(max. 10 participants)

Looking for a safe space where you can share your thoughts and challenges with other like-valued members of the Redefining S.E.L.F.I.S.H. community?

This 60-minute small-group discussion is a deep-dive on one element of the model. You'll hear others' perspectives and gain further guidance for successful implementation in your life.

**Please note:** It is a pre-requisite of your participation in this session that you have read the Redefining S.E.L.F.I.S.H. book and completed all the associated activities.

## 1-2-1 session:
## Single S.E.L.F.I.S.H. element
A 90-minute bespoke session where I will guide you in-depth through your choice of element of the S.E.L.F.I.S.H. model, looking at your aims and challenges. Together we will cement

the changes you want to make to prioritise you. Session includes a Q&A opportunity for maximum impact on your life.

## 1-2-1 programme:
## All S.E.L.F.I.S.H. elements
## NO NEED TO READ / RE-READ THE BOOK!

Looking for a short-cut to Redefining S.E.L.F.I.S.H.? Want optimum results that fit around your busy life?

Then this deluxe option is perfect for you! No need to read the book.

Work 1-2-1 with Carolyn through the entire model at your pace. Gain additional insights and bespoke coaching in a programme designed especially for you and your life.

## Carolyn's programmes designed just for you!

To access the full list of Carolyn's courses please visit www.carolynhobdey.com.

Courses range from 4 to 12 weeks dependent on initial consultation.

### From Falling to Flying: How to recover from setbacks and failure

Have things not gone your way lately? At work? At home?

Failure can be hard, but the ability to handle setbacks is a skill you can develop and utilise throughout your life. In this series you'll build the confidence to bounce back and reframe failures from negative to positive.

### From Boredom to Buzzing: How to rediscover your love of life

Are you just going through the motions? Does your life feel a bit lacklustre?

If you'd like to get back your passion for life, then this series will help you find your mojo and achieve a life well-lived.

### From Guilt to Great: How to stop feeling bad and start feeling fabulous

Do you beat yourself up about stuff? Do you harbour guilt or regret?

In this series I'll help free you from those feelings and begin living life with positivity – about you and what you're capable of.

**From Self-loathing to Self-love: How to improve your relationship with you**

Do you suffer from low self-worth? Would you like to love you more?

The longest relationship we ever have is the one we have with ourselves, so why not make it the best relationship? In this series I help you to examine the negative stories you tell yourself and become your own best friend.

**From Hot Flush to Hot Stuff: How to regain your mojo after the menopause**

Has the menopause damaged your self-esteem? Are you feeling foggy, frumpy or fed-up?

Having endured a premature menopause, I know exactly how that feels. I'm here to tell you that it doesn't have to stay that way. 'The Change' can mean positive change for you!

NOTES

NOTES

NOTES

NOTES

NOTES

NOTES